This book was purchased with funds generously donated by

<u>Ms. Joyce Marlin</u>

In addition to being a sponsor to our 2nd Annual Fun Run/Walk, Joyce was Senior Branch Librarian at the Concord Library from 1979—1993

Lemurs

Tree Dwellers

by Erika L. Shores

Consultant:
Ian Tattersall, PhD
Curator, Division of Anthropology
American Museum of Natural History, New York City
author, *Primates: Lemurs, Monkeys, and You*

Bridgestone Books
an imprint of Capstone Press
Mankato, Minnesota

Bridgestone Books are published by Capstone Press
151 Good Counsel Drive, P.O. Box 669, Mankato, Minnesota 56002
www.capstonepress.com

Library of Congress Cataloging-in-Publication Data
Shores, Erika L., 1976–
    Lemurs: tree dwellers / by Erika L. Shores.
    p. cm.—(The wild world of animals)
    Includes bibliographical references (p. 24) and index.
    ISBN 0-7368-2614-9 (hardcover)
    1. Lemurs—Juvenile literature. [1. Lemurs.] I. Title. II. Series.
QL737.P95 S56 2005
599.8'3—dc22   2003024900

Summary: An introduction to the physical characteristics, behaviors, habitats, and life
    cycles of lemurs.

Editorial Credits
Roberta Schmidt, editor; Linda Clavel, designer; Scott Thoms, photo researcher;
    Eric Kudalis, product planning editor

Photo Credits
Corbis/John Garrett, 20
Digital Vision, 1
Index Stock Imagery/John Dominis, 12
Lynn M. Stone, cover, 8
Minden Pictures/Frans Lanting, 6; Mitsuaki Iwago, 4
Nature Picture Library/Pete Oxford, 16
PhotoDisc Inc., 14
Tom & Pat Leeson, 18
Wolfgang Kaehler/www.wkaehlerphoto.com, 10

1 2 3 4 5 6 09 08 07 06 05 04

Table of Contents

FUN FACTS

Lemurs use their long bushy tails for balancing when they jump from branch to branch in trees.

Coquerel's dwarf lemur

Lemurs

Lemurs are small furry animals. There are about 50 kinds of lemurs. Most lemurs have big eyes and long bushy tails. Some lemurs have black, white, or gray fur. Other lemurs are brown, red, or tan. Lemurs can be as small as mice or larger than house cats.

Lemurs have thumbs. Their thumbs help them pick up objects with their hands.

ring-tailed lemurs

6

Lemurs Are Primates

Lemurs are **primates**. Primates are a kind of **mammal**. People and monkeys also are primates. Primates have eyes that face forward. They use their hands to grasp things. Lemurs use their hands to grasp food and tree branches.

red-ruffed lemur

Where Lemurs Live

Lemurs live on islands near Africa. Most lemurs live on the island of Madagascar. Some lemurs live on the Comoro Islands. Lemur habitats include rain forests and dry areas. Lemurs spend most of their time in trees or spiny plants.

habitat
the place and natural conditions in which an animal lives

indri

10

What Lemurs Eat

Most lemurs eat only leaves, fruits, and flowers. These lemurs are **herbivores**. They use their thumbs and fingers to pull leaves and fruits off trees. Some lemurs also eat insects. These lemurs are **omnivores**.

FUN FACTS

Ring-tailed lemurs sometimes have stink fights. They shake their smelly tails at each other.

ring-tailed lemurs

Scents

Lemurs can use scents to communicate with each other. Lemurs mark the ground and tree branches with their scents. A male ring-tailed lemur shakes his tail to spread his scent through the air. The scent tells other lemurs to stay away.

communicate

to share information, ideas, or feelings

FUN FACTS

Most sifakas are born in August or September.

sifakas

14

Mating and Birth

A male and female lemur mate to produce young. A female lemur gives birth to a young lemur between two and five months later. Some kinds of lemurs give birth to two or more young. Some female lemurs give birth to their young in a nest.

mate
to join together to produce young

ring-tailed lemurs

Lemur Infants

Young lemurs are called infants. Many infant lemurs cling to their mothers' stomachs. After about two to four weeks, infant lemurs often ride on their mothers' backs. Infants drink their mothers' milk for about two months.

FUN FACTS

Red-ruffed lemurs have at least 12 different calls that warn of danger.

red-ruffed lemur

Predators

Some animals hunt lemurs. Eagles, snakes, and fossas kill lemurs for food. Some lemurs make loud noises to warn each other when a **predator** is near. These noises sound like screams or yells. Lemurs move to a safer place when they hear these noises.

fossa
a slender, catlike animal that lives in Madagascar

mouse lemur

Lemurs and People

People are the biggest danger to lemurs. Some people kill lemurs for food. Other people destroy lemur habitats. They cut down trees to build homes, roads, and farms.

Some people work to save lemurs. National parks in Madagascar help protect areas where lemurs live.

Hands On: Lemur Hands

Lemurs and humans use their thumbs to help them pick up objects. A human can pick up an object by using one finger and one thumb. A lemur cannot use its fingers separately. A lemur must use all of its fingers with its thumb to grasp objects. Try this activity to see how your hand is different from a lemur's hand.

What You Need

paper clips
pencil
paper
masking tape

What You Do

1. Place the paper clips, pencil, and paper on a table.
2. Use a piece of masking tape to tape the fingers of your left hand together.
3. Try to pick up the objects on the table with your left hand.
4. Now, pick up the objects with your right hand. You can use just your thumb and index finger to pick up the objects on the table.

Was it easier to pick up the objects using your thumb and index finger?

Glossary

herbivore (HUR-buh-vor)—an animal that eats only plants

mammal (MAM-uhl)—a warm-blooded animal with a backbone and hair; female mammals produce milk to feed their young.

omnivore (OM-nuh-vor)—an animal that eats plants and other animals

predator (PRED-uh-tur)—an animal that hunts other animals for food

primate (PRYE-mate)—any animal in the group of mammals that includes humans, apes, and monkeys; primates use their fingers and thumbs to hold objects.

Read More

Butz, Christopher. *Lemurs.* Animals of the Rain Forest. Austin, Texas: Raintree Steck-Vaughn, 2002.

Martin, Patricia A. Fink. *Lemurs, Lorises, and Other Lower Primates.* A True Book. New York: Children's Press, 2000.

Powzyk, Joyce Ann. *A Little Lemur Named Mew.* Brookfield, Conn.: Millbrook Press, 2003.

Internet Sites

FactHound offers a safe, fun way to find Internet sites related to this book. All of the sites on FactHound have been researched by our staff.

Here's how:
1. Visit *www.facthound.com*
2. Type in this special code **0736826149** for age-appropriate sites. Or enter a search word related to this book for a more general search.
3. Click on the **Fetch It** button.

FactHound will fetch the best sites for you!

Index